A Game

by Zoey Young
illustrated by John Olmos

Practice Pre-Decodable 13

Mc Graw Hill Education

Bothell, WA • Chicago, IL • Columbus, OH • New York, NY

MHEonline.com

Send all inquiries to:
McGraw-Hill Education
8787 Orion Place
Columbus, OH 43240

ISBN: 978-0-02-141257-0
MHID: 0-02-141257-X

Printed in China.

9 10 11 12 13 DSS 27 26 25 24 23

We had  .

caps

We had 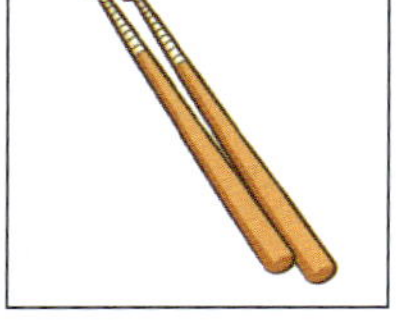 .

bats

We had 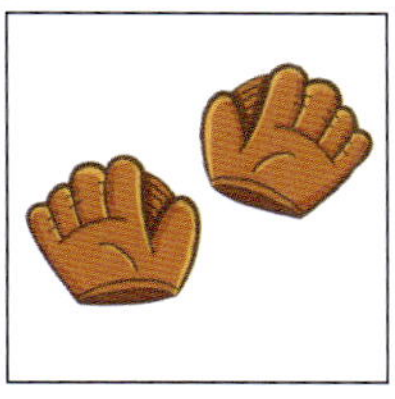.

gloves

We had a  .

helmet

We had a 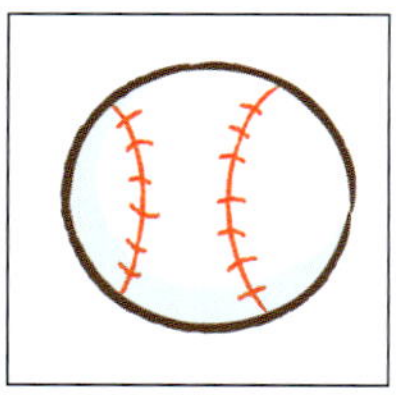 !

baseball

We had a 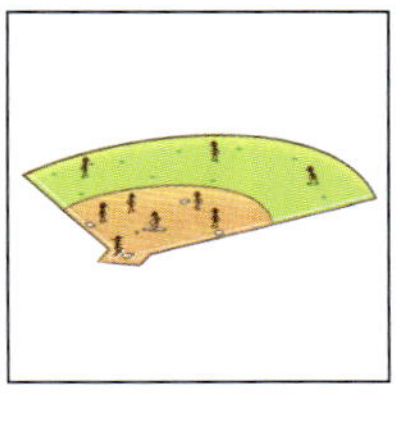 !

game